Accept the challenge

B

Believe in the cause

C

Choice not chance
determines success

D

Define yourself and develop
your own goals and objectives

E

Expect failure but
also expect success

F

Fight on, be faithful
and finish what you start

G

Gravitate towards
positive people doing great things

H

Harness your energies
to be successful

Initiate the process
to get involved and learn how to

J

Jealousy gets you nowhere
but you must always justify your actions

Keep on keepin' on and kick those negative habits and folks to the curb

Learn how to learn so you
learn something new everyday

M

Measure your worth by what's
inside your head and heart

Never, never, never say never

O

Organize your life
and order your steps

P

Put first things first,
but always practice what it is you preach

Quit quitting; quitters
never win and winners never quit

R

Respect people based upon
their skills, talents and achievements

S

Stay strong to your values and beliefs

T

Travel the long road to equality...
we still have a long way to go

U

Utilize your network
or someone else's to do well in life

V

Visualize it!
Only when you see it
can you be it

Work, work, work, work,
work till all your work is done

X-ray your own life
for improvement

Yield to opportunity

Zealously strive to achieve

Compelling thoughts
from the inspirational mind of SPKR4LIFE,
Byron V. Garrett

Find something in life that you love doing that you'd do it for free,
but do it so well you get paid for it.

You have 24 hours in a day — 12 hours to mind your business, 12 hours to take care
of your business which leaves you ZERO time for anybody else's business.
X-ray your own life for improvement.

You must be willing to do today what others won't do to have tomorrow
what others never will.

There are three sides to every issue:
yours, mine and the one we've yet to consider.

Being a man or woman is a matter of birth but being a man or woman
who makes a difference is a matter of choice. Choose to make a difference.

Byron V. Garrett

One of the most compelling voices of our time. Byron V. Garrett is Chairman of the National Family Engagement Alliance and leads education leadership & policy for Microsoft. Byron serves as an education blogger for The Huffington Post and is a consulting author for Scholastic. The former CEO of the National PTA, Byron has advised government agencies, Fortune 500 companies, education organizations, celebrities and professional athletes. A leading education advocate, Byron served as a key strategist for NBC News' Education Nation and produced the 1st Annual Building A Grad Nation Summit for the America's Promise Alliance. In addition, Byron is a former K-8 Principal and served as Co-Convener of the Helping America's Youth Initiative for The White House. Byron is the author of the highly popular, The ABC's of Life (Scholastic 2013) and There's Greatness on the Inside (Life Works Press 2015).

For additional copies, resources or information,
please visit: www.abcsoflife.com